DAVID BECKHAM

2003 ANNUAL

£5.99

ZINC 7

Published by Zincseven Limited
City Forum
250 City Road
London EC1 2QO

Printed in the E.U.

Contents

6

Introduction

If film-star Arnold Schwarzenegger is the muscle-bound All-American Hero, then David Beckham, the equally famous England football captain, is a different kind of role model altogether. As a sportsman, he's in a league of his own, with a leadership style more understated than the up-and-at-'em, all guns blazing stereotype – but one that seems to have inspired both a team and a nation. Add his high-flying lifestyle, including a fleet of sports cars, a pop-star wife and the country's most famous toddler, Brooklyn, and it's clear you're talking about nothing less than a phenomenon.

It wasn't always like this, though. Back in June 1998, when he was sent off for kicking out at an Argentine opponent, he was the most hated public figure in the land. He couldn't step on a football pitch anywhere without becoming the target for yobbish abuse. Yet four years on, the nation worship this man. This is Beckham's story.

FACTFILE

Full Name: David Robert Joseph Beckham
Date of Birth: 2 May 1975
Place of Birth: Leytonstone, London
Height: 180 cm (5ft 11in)
Hair: Blond
Marital status: Married to Victoria
Clubs: Manchester United,
          Preston North End (loan in 1995)

On the Pitch

2001-2002

Beckham - match by match

Sun 12 Aug v Liverpool Charity Shield Cardiff	1-2	A gentle curtain-raiser at the Millennium Stadium? Not where these two clubs were concerned! But David failed to make his mark in a narrow defeat made all the more galling by a second-minute conceded penalty.
Sun 19 Aug v Fulham League Home	3-2	A trademark free-kick opened David and United's account for the season in a live television game that, with upstarts Fulham leading twice, had the viewing millions on the edge of their seats.
Wed 22 Aug v Blackburn R League Away	2-2	Two goals for Becks at Ewood Park as their newly promoted Lancashire rivals took a point against the Champions. Becks' late free kick spared United's blushes.
Sun 26 Aug v Aston Villa League Away	1-1	David was substituted by Andy Cole in the 70th minute of this second consecutive away draw, which saw United face a returning Peter Schmeichel. The last-minute equaliser was a Villa own goal.
Sat 8 Sep v Everton League Home	4-1	Coming on as sub in the 77th minute with the game already won, David notched a last-gasp goal to seal an emphatic victory. This sent United second behind surprise leaders Bolton.
Sat 15 Sep v Newcastle U League Away	3-4	A thrilling match for the uncommitted saw United and David go down to the odd goal in seven, giving notice of the Magpies' title aspirations.
Tues 18 Sep v Lille European Cup Home	1-0	David celebrated the first game in United's defence of their European crown with a last-minute winner against French opposition.
Tues 25 Sep v Deportivo European Cup Away	1-2	Having been rested for Saturday's League game, David was a late sub in Portugal but had no time to affect the result.
Sat 29 Sep v Tottenham H League Away	5-3	David received his first yellow card of the season, but more importantly made an 87th-minute goal as Tottenham are crushed on their own turf. United now just two points behind leaders Arsenal.

Wed 10 Oct **v Olympiakos** **European Cup** **Away**	2-0	Unwilling to be rested after helping England qualify for the World Cup, Becks hits another wondergoal in a memorable United awayday and ensured they go clear at the top of their group.
Wed 17 Oct **v Deportivo** **European Cup** **Home**	2-3	A second European reverse, at home against Deportivo, but this time United and David go down fighting.
Tues 23 Oct **v Olympiakos** **European Cup** **Home**	3-0	Back (or should that be Beck?) on track as United do the double over the Greeks in emphatic fashion. They must be fed up with David by now!
Sat 27 Oct **v Leeds U** **League** **Home**	1-1	A yellow card, David's second, as bitter rivals United (currently fifth in the table) and second-placed Leeds contested a hard-fought draw in front of a rabid 67,555 crowd.
Tues 31 Oct **v Lille** **European Cup** **Away**	1-1	A hard-fought away draw in northern France, David digging in to play his part in an all-round gutsy performance.
Sun 4 Nov **v Liverpool** **League** **Away**	1-3	David scored in the 50th minute but left the action 13 minutes before the end – as did many United fans in the 45,000 crowd. A defeat to United's rivals was, sadly, already on the cards.
Sat 17 Nov **v Leicester C** **League** **Home**	2-0	An easy victory against a team already looking out of their depth in the top flight in front of an Old Trafford full house of 67,651.
Tues 20 Nov **v Bayern M** **European Cup** **Away**	1-1	United's final European match before the winter break saw them return from Germany with a satisfactory point – though at 1-0 up with five minutes to go, a win looked the more likely outcome.
Sun 25 Nov **v Arsenal** **League** **Away**	1-3	A caution was a small price to pay as the Red Devils leave their Championship rivals with a bloody nose.
Sat 1 Dec **v Chelsea** **League** **Home**	0-3	A day on which everything went wrong. David was withdrawn a quarter of an hour before the whistle, and few of the 67,544 present went home happy.
Sat 8 Dec **v West Ham** **League** **Home**	0-1	First of a run of three sub appearances for David, but his entry after an hour could not save the game. Now in ninth place (under newcomers Fulham!), United needed his magic more than ever.

Sat 22 Dec v Southampton League Home	6-1	An almost embarrassing rout of struggling Southampton saw David introduced for a stroll with 25 minutes left.
Wed 26 Dec v Everton League Away	2-0	Warming the bench again, David made his entrance ten minutes after the interval, and United left Merseyside with all three points.
Sun 30 Dec v Fulham League Away	3-2	A fourth yellow card of the season as United eased past Premiership new boys Fulham in a match that packed ancient Craven Cottage to the rafters. 21,159 was their best attendance of the season despite the Sky cameras.
Wed 2 Jan v Newcastle U League Home	3-1	Revenge for last year's beating at St James's was extracted without too much help from David, an 85th-minute substitute. United now lay a threatening second behind Leeds.
Sun 6 Jan v Aston Villa FA Cup Away	3-2	David's first and only FA Cup match of the campaign saw Villa (and Schmeichel) put to the sword by the odd goal in five. Dramatically, United's three came in five second-half minutes.
Sun 13 Jan v Southampton League Away	3-1	United prefer St Mary's to the Dell, and David registered his own vote with a goal in first-half injury time. A comfortable win in front of nearly 32,000 – including a large number of Reds.
Sat 19 Jan v Blackburn R League Home	2-1	A less than convincing win thanks to a Ruud penalty and late Roy Keane strike. A quiet game – but with United top of the table by two points from Newcastle, few of the 67,552 present cared!
Tues 22 Jan v Liverpool League Home	0-1	David was withdrawn late on in a disappointing game that saw Liverpool score the season's first league double against United. It seemed Fergie's imminent retirement was causing collywobbles.
Tues 29 Jan v Bolton W League Away	4-0	The shortest journey for an away game saw United return with the points and a healthy boost to their goal difference thanks to Solskjaer (hat trick) and Van Nistelrooy.
Sat 2 Feb v Sunderland League Home	4-1	The second goal in a rout of the Wearsiders fell to United's Number 7, restoring the lead after a rare Phil Neville strike. A brace from the Ruud boy did the rest, and United were snugly in second place.
Sun 10 Feb v Charlton League Away	2-0	The Valley proved a happy hunting ground with a Solskjaer goal in either half. United now two points and 11 goals clear at the top from Liverpool. And Fergie was staying on – what more could be asked?

Wed 20 Feb v Nantes European Cup Away	1-1	Behind after eight minutes, United had to wait until added time before being awarded a penalty. Ruud van Nistelrooy stepped forward to take the spot kick and coolly put it away. United top of their group on goal difference.
Sat 23 Feb v Aston Villa League Home	1-0	A rather quiet (not to mention windy) third meeting of the season with the Midlanders, and another mid-day kick-off, was settled by a second half Van Nistelrooy goal giving United 12 wins in 13 games.
Tues 26 Feb v Nantes European Cup Home	5-1	An 18th-minute humdinger of a Becks free-kick set United on the way to their most emphatic European win yet. That said, visitors Nantes had the audacity to hit the bar and score first!
Sun 3 Mar v Derby C League Away	2-2	A hard-fought draw at the home of relegation strugglers Derby saw United, bidding for a Premiership record seven straight away wins, lose ground against Arsenal – now one point behind but with a game in hand.
Wed 6 Mar v Tottenham H League Home	4-0	Glenn's men see United notch nine over their two games. David registers one in each half to add to Hod's headache. 67,599 were present, one of United's top gates of the season.
Wed 13 Mar v Bayern M European Cup Home	0-0	Points dropped that would happily not prevent United progressing to the semi-final stage of Europe's top competition. Which, without Becks, would be as far as they got.
Sat 16 Mar v West Ham League Away	5-3	A stunning away win, marked by two Beckham goals in the 17th and 89th minutes. The first equalised an opening Hammer blow, the latter a coolly taken penalty that put the icing on the cake. He played a part in the other three, too!
Tues 19 Mar v Boavista European Cup Away	3-0	A package holiday to Portugal sees Boavista packed off with a three-goal burst. David contributed the last, a 51st-minute penalty, after finding Laurent Blanc's head with a pinpoint corner for the opener. All too easy.
Sat 23 Mar v Middlesbrough League Home	0-1	Former assistant boss Steve McClaren's return to Old Trafford wasn't a happy one for United, who yielded the points, or Becks, who reached the five-caution disciplinary landmark during this defeat.
Sat 30 Mar v Leeds U League Away	4-3	An epic win at Elland Road in a mid-day match, the highlight a pinpoint cross for Ryan Giggs' fourth, couldn't be marred by a sixth yellow card of the season. United's 9th win in the last 13 clashes, and unbeaten in four at Elland Road.

Tues 2 Apr v Deportivo European Cup Home	2-0	The third meeting between the clubs this season brought United's first victory – how satisfying was that? David was subbed in the last minute when the work was done.
Tues 9 Apr v Deportivo European Cup Away	3-2	The match in which tragedy struck. A bone-breaking 21st-minute challenge by Argentinean player Pedro Duscher saw Becks stretchered out of the game…and the World Cup?

Season

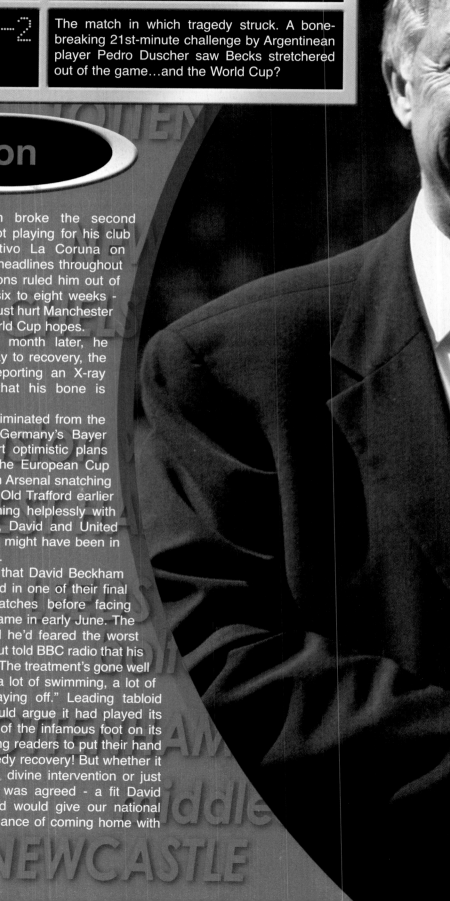

When David Beckham broke the second metatarsal in his left foot playing for his club against Spain's Deportivo La Coruna on 9 April, the event made headlines throughout the world. Initial predictions ruled him out of competitive football for six to eight weeks - something that wouldn't just hurt Manchester United but England's World Cup hopes. Thankfully, less than a month later, he appeared well on the way to recovery, the club's official website reporting an X-ray which showed "signs that his bone is healing satisfactorily".

Sadly, United were eliminated from the Champions League by Germany's Bayer Leverkusen, cutting short optimistic plans for Becks to return for the European Cup Final on 15 May. And with Arsenal snatching the Double with a win at Old Trafford earlier that month, Becks watching helplessly with Victoria from the stands, David and United could only dream of what might have been in a rare trophy-less season.

But hopes were high that David Beckham could turn out for England in one of their final World Cup warm-up matches before facing Sweden in the opening game in early June. The England captain admitted he'd feared the worst after breaking the bone, but told BBC radio that his recovery was going well. "The treatment's gone well this week and I've done a lot of swimming, a lot of weight work, and it's paying off." Leading tabloid newspaper 'The Sun' would argue it had played its part by printing a picture of the infamous foot on its front page and encouraging readers to put their hand on it and pray for his speedy recovery! But whether it was down to expert help, divine intervention or just mother nature, everyone was agreed - a fit David Beckham leading England would give our national team the best possible chance of coming home with the World Cup.

Becks and manager Alex Ferguson shake hands to confirm another 3 years with United.

Rise to Stardom

The birth of a son, David Robert Joseph, to Ted and Sandra Beckham on 2nd May 1975, was a happy occasion. But the birth was nowhere near Manchester, but in Leytonstone, East London. The local football teams were West Ham and Orient, while David's grandfather was a Tottenham season-ticket holder, but the youngster supported his father's team of choice.

Ted had played non-league football to a reasonable standard, and was involved in managing a local Sunday league side. David started accompanying him to games and, once the game was over, would happily take his turn on the pitch kicking around with his Dad. Fortunately, Ted Beckham was not a father who sought to achieve his own unfulfilled ambitions through his son. "He has never been a father that shouts and swears at you from the side of the pitch," David has said. "He's one of my fiercest critics, but we've got respect for each other. He wasn't a pushy father."

David went to the local Roger Norman soccer school, a fistful of badges evidence of his early prowess, and as soon as he was old enough he joined a local boys' team called Ridgeway Rovers. It was when they won a five-a-side tournament that David picked up the first of many press cuttings.

Next stop on his journey to fame was winning a nationwide competition organised by the Bobby Charlton soccer school. Sir Bobby (as he is now) was a Manchester United hero of the '60s and had played in England's World Cup-winning team of 1966, so he was clearly a great role model for any up-and-coming young footballer. David won his regional heat and went on to show off his skills in front of a capacity Old Trafford crowd as part of the pre-match entertainment – in December 1986. His prize was a two-week trip to Barcelona, then managed by Terry Venables – the first of many overseas assignments, as it would turn out. In 1987, David made another appearance in front of the United fans as mascot for the away game at West Ham – not a million miles away from his home.

Even at this early stage, David knew he was destined for greatness. "I remember writing my name out over and over again when I was at school," he now admits, "just in case I ever became famous!" Having first tried out with Leyton Orient, he would go training with Tottenham at their School of Excellence alongside Jamie Redknapp, a player who would also play for England and marry a pop star – in his case, ex-Eternal stunner Louise Nurding. As for an alternative career had his sporting ambitions not worked out, David really hasn't a clue. "I've always enjoyed

Becks in the early days playing for Manchester United.

drawing, so maybe something to do with art. But football was always what I wanted to do."

Having impressed in the Theatre of Dreams (as Old Trafford is known), it was no surprise that the club kept tabs on the talented youngster, and one day, after he'd turned out for Waltham Forest Under 12s against Redbridge, United's London scout paid a call on the family. They wanted to sign David when he left school – and though Spurs (and, it's rumoured, neighbours Arsenal) also offered him terms, there was only one choice. Sorry, Grandad! The next few years at Chingford High School were spent in a blur as he counted the months away to the day he could be a full-time footballer.

The deed was done in July 1991, David travelling north to stay in 'digs' with Tony and Annie Kay, a kindly couple with whom he would develop almost a parent-son relationship over the coming years. For a boy who'd grown up in the 'soft south', though, the move to Manchester was a culture shock. "It was like stepping into Coronation Street," he'd rather untactfully comment years later. "It's a daunting feeling when you're 16, leaving home and coming up to a strange place."

But that strange place was where he had been born to be. "Stepping onto the pitch at Old Trafford gives you goosebumps," he'd say, describing it as "one of the best feelings ever." He won an honour in his very first season at United, playing for the team that won the FA Youth Cup in May 1992 by beating Crystal Palace 6-3. As he was to find out, though, not everything would come that easy.

Having won the Youth Cup, United started the next season as favourites to retain it, but would lose 4-1 in the Final to Leeds United – despite the presence of Paul Scholes and Gary Neville alongside David in the team. But David had already had a taste of the big time, coming on as substitute while still a trainee professional in a Rumbelows (now Worthington) Cup tie at lowly Brighton in September 1992. He would sign full professional forms four months later.

Yet the competition for first-team places was so intense that he wouldn't get another chance for two years – September 1994, again in the League Cup and again against lower-division opposition in Port Vale. Better was to come as he scored his first goal for the club. Unfortunately it was on a disappointing night for United, as they were knocked out of Europe despite beating Galatasaray in the Champions League. David, though, will never forget scoring in front of the 38,301 fans present at Old Trafford – even if it was back to the reserves afterwards.

Just when he was beginning to despair of his first-team future, David was summoned to the office of manager Alex Ferguson – a rare occurrence for someone so young and relatively untried – in March 1995. And the news he received rocked him back on his heels: 'Fergie' was asking him to leave Old Trafford! Happily, it was only a temporary assignment at Third Division Preston North End. And far from signalling the end of the road for the player, it was a chance to gain some much-needed League experience.

It was a bit of a culture shock, too, for the players at Deepdale didn't have the same level of creature comforts as their Old Trafford counterparts – they even had to wash their own muddy kit! Luckily David coped, and scored two goals in the five matches he played in Preston white. (The first came in his debut against Doncaster Rovers, having come on as a second-half substitute.) More than that, he claimed man-of-the-match honours three times, and it was hardly

David has been a huge influence on United ever since he broke into the team in 1996, after the departure of Andrei Kanchelskis.

David in action against
Liverpool in the 1996
FA Cup Final.

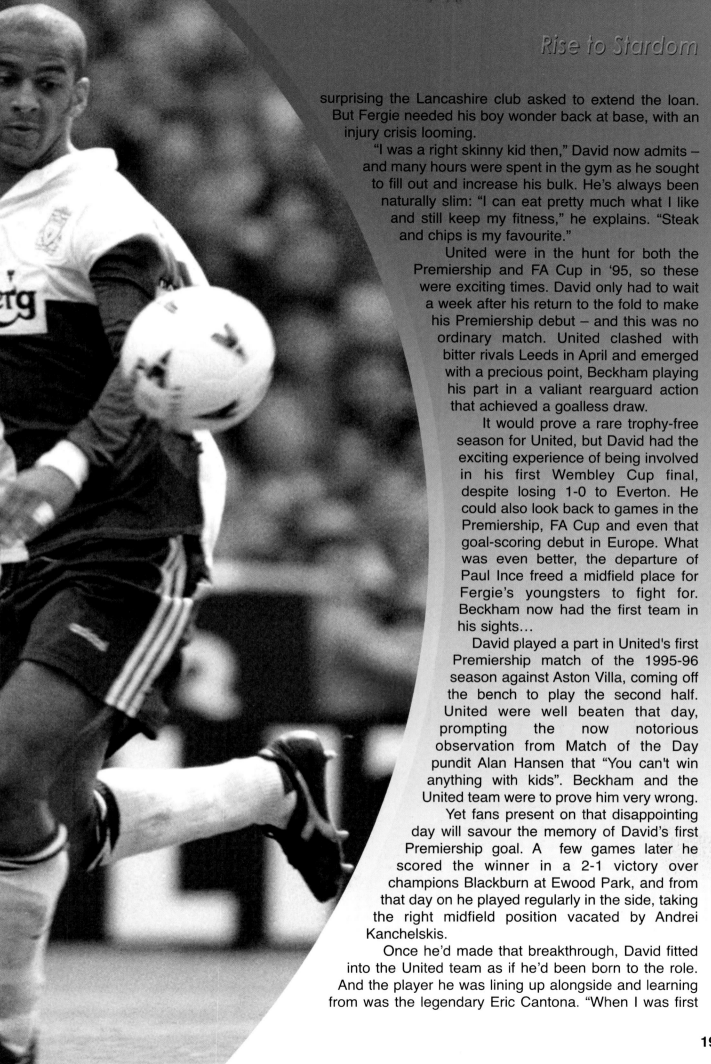

surprising the Lancashire club asked to extend the loan. But Fergie needed his boy wonder back at base, with an injury crisis looming.

"I was a right skinny kid then," David now admits – and many hours were spent in the gym as he sought to fill out and increase his bulk. He's always been naturally slim: "I can eat pretty much what I like and still keep my fitness," he explains. "Steak and chips is my favourite."

United were in the hunt for both the Premiership and FA Cup in '95, so these were exciting times. David only had to wait a week after his return to the fold to make his Premiership debut – and this was no ordinary match. United clashed with bitter rivals Leeds in April and emerged with a precious point, Beckham playing his part in a valiant rearguard action that achieved a goalless draw.

It would prove a rare trophy-free season for United, but David had the exciting experience of being involved in his first Wembley Cup final, despite losing 1-0 to Everton. He could also look back to games in the Premiership, FA Cup and even that goal-scoring debut in Europe. What was even better, the departure of Paul Ince freed a midfield place for Fergie's youngsters to fight for. Beckham now had the first team in his sights...

David played a part in United's first Premiership match of the 1995-96 season against Aston Villa, coming off the bench to play the second half. United were well beaten that day, prompting the now notorious observation from Match of the Day pundit Alan Hansen that "You can't win anything with kids". Beckham and the United team were to prove him very wrong.

Yet fans present on that disappointing day will savour the memory of David's first Premiership goal. A few games later he scored the winner in a 2-1 victory over champions Blackburn at Ewood Park, and from that day on he played regularly in the side, taking the right midfield position vacated by Andrei Kanchelskis.

Once he'd made that breakthrough, David fitted into the United team as if he'd been born to the role. And the player he was lining up alongside and learning from was the legendary Eric Cantona. "When I was first

In action against
Middlesbrough which
wrapped the 1996 title for
United.

told I was playing in the first team, Eric gave me advice on where to play and what to do," he explains, "and that really helped. I was dead chuffed, thinking 'Wow, Eric has talked to me!'"

The unlikely duo powered the Red Devils past Newcastle to reclaim the Premiership crown, despite Keegan's Magpies having a 12-point lead at one stage, while at Wembley against Liverpool it was David's inswinging corner that set up who else but Cantona for the game's only goal. With 33 League appearances (seven goals) and three more Cup games, David Beckham had arrived. And England was clearly the next step.

David had already represented his country nine times at Under-21 level. But when national coach Glenn Hoddle included the player in his squad for the World Cup qualifier in Moldova, his memory had undoubtedly been jogged by one of the most audacious goals ever seen on TV. David had lobbed Wimbledon's Scots international keeper Neil Sullivan from the half-way line in the opening game of the 1996-97 season (having already scored in the Charity Shield defeat of Newcastle), ensuring Hoddle could hardly leave him out!

David had just turned 21 and, though he'd had girlfriends, no-one had rivalled the game of football for his affections. Until, while in Georgia with England late in 1996, he was relaxing with room-mate Gary Neville and saw the Spice Girls video 'Say You'll Be There' on the television. Fixing his Manchester United club-mate with a determined stare, he said: "That's the girl for me, and I am going to get her."

The object of his attention was, of course, Victoria Adams, alias Posh Spice. And coincidentally his path would cross that of the glamorous pop star soon after his return to Britain. With her then-boyfriend Stuart Bilton recovering after a skiing accident, Victoria was invited to see Manchester United play at Chelsea. The pair spotted each other across the crowded players lounge at Stamford Bridge but, frustratingly, were unable to strike up a conversation. It was when her fellow Spice Girl Mel C suggested going to watch Manchester United in action against Sheffield Wednesday that the pair were finally able to talk. The attraction for both parties was immediate.

The pair had a lot in common because although Victoria's knowledge of football was slim, she, like David was used to being the centre of attention the moment she walked in a room. Both knew the price of fame, and though their relationship would turn them into the most talked-about couple since Prince Charles and Princess Diana, they were willing to face that challenge. It would prove as demanding as anything either had had to face in their respective careers to date.

David's fan mail had already been up to 200 letters a week before he got together with Victoria, and that total was soon to shoot skywards as he found his face in 'Smash Hits' as often as the sports pages. Suddenly Top Shop wanted him to model clothes, while Brylcreem signed him up as the man most likely to sell hair-care products. His floppy fringe would become something of a trademark until it was replaced by the shaven-headed look.

DB

The Ups and Downs

David's 1996-97 season was an up and down story. Though his own sparkling form would win him the coveted accolade of PFA Young Player of the Year, his club side would only come out of it with one trophy. That was, however, the Premiership – their fourth win in five years. And the England situation was even rosier, as a defeat by Italy was reversed when they won in Poland. Unfortunately, two bookings in a friendly tournament in France meant David missed out on the chance to face World Champions Brazil, but he, along with millions of England fans, must have been hoping he'd be lining up against them in France 12 months later.

His relationship with Victoria was coming along fast and furious, even though they'd taken four dates to share their first kiss! The summer of 1998 would see them sharing a rare few days of quality time together in New York (where their son, Brooklyn, was conceived!). But that followed on from a World Cup campaign which had started so promisingly for David yet would leave him desolate.

United's 1997-98 season had been equally disappointing. They'd been so far ahead of the pack in March that one Manchester bookmaker even paid out to people who'd bet on them securing the title. Unfortunately, Londoners Arsenal put together an unbeaten run dating from December that would only be broken after they'd wrestled the crown from the Red Devils by a single point. In Europe, United fell to Jean Tigana's Monaco, while the FA Cup trail fizzled out at lowly Barnsley.

David was left with England as his only hope of glory, so there was more than just national pride at stake as he jetted out to France with the rest of the team for the World Cup Finals. He'd made his first full international appearance in a World Cup qualifying game, and was the only player to have started every one. After securing the draw in Rome that booked their ticket, England had believed they could live with the best. But David was left out of the first game, coach Hoddle deciding he "wasn't focused enough". He did however come on against Romania as a

David celebrates his first goal for England against Columbia in the World Cup '98.

A tragic moment in David's career - receiving a red card during the Argentina match at World Cup '98.

substitute, but defeat in that game left England needing a win to go through and face Argentina in the second round. Cometh the hour, cometh the man – and David showed the waiting world (and Glenn Hoddle) a thing or two when he bent a trademark free-kick round the Colombian wall to set up a dream tie with Argentina.

Unfortunately, the clash with the South Americans was hyped up by the press on two fronts – memories of the Falklands War and the 1986 clash in Mexico which was won by two goals from superstar Diego Maradona. The first goal included the infamous 'Hand of God' incident where he'd punched the ball past Peter Shilton. The first half began with a penalty for the Argentines, equalised by Shearer, before David fed the ball to teenage prodigy Michael Owen. His run, covering half the pitch, preceded a memorable goal that put him on the international map and England ahead in the game. A late Argentine equaliser set up the second half for a feast of football.

Unfortunately, what the game would be remembered for was not the football but David Beckham's sending-off, flicking a petulant foot out at Diego Simeone under the eagle eye of the referee. It was a moment he would regret forever – but, even though he'd been fouled and had his hair pulled by the opponent in a gesture supposed to be an apologetic ruffling of the hair, he became the villain of the piece due to a childish moment of temper. It was the first dismissal of his professional career. And if his long walk to the dressing room was a saddening experience, England's departure from the competition on penalties after extra time was equally heartbreaking.

David proved he was a man by shouldering the blame fairly and squarely. "This is without doubt the worst moment of my career," he said. "I will always regret my actions. I have apologised to the England players and management and I want every England supporter to know how deeply sorry I am. I only hope that I will have the opportunity in the future to be part of a successful England team in the European Championships and World Cup."

Those final words would prove prophetic indeed – but the media storm that followed in '98 was astonishing. The entire burden of blame for England exiting the competition was laid not at the feet of Ince and Batty, the players who missed the penalties, but David Beckham. His parents' house was staked out by press photographers, and when he flew to New York to be with Victoria, who was touring the States with the Spice Girls, he had to be smuggled though the kitchens at Heathrow Airport to avoid being spotted. Talk about out of the frying pan! It was even rumoured the pressure would force him out of Old Trafford and into a big-money move abroad, an idea quickly scotched by Alex Ferguson.

Nevertheless he had to run the gauntlet of opposing fans, starting at West Ham's compact Upton Park ground in August 1998 when his every touch of the ball was jeered at the closest of close quarters. Chants would become ever more disgusting, to the point where he was pictured making a V-sign to Leeds United fans. Yet that was a rare moment of weakness from a man who admitted in a 1999 TV documentary that "more people dislike me than like me."

But events in his private life were to make David Beckham's outlook far happier. He and Victoria had got engaged in January 1998, when she had made him get down on bended knee a second time so she could re-live the moment! He gave her a £40,000 diamond ring, while his was a 'mere' £15,000 trinket. That summer, he was snapped wearing a skirt-like

David lifts the European Cup in '99 after defeating German side Bayern Munich.

The happy couple
shortly before their
wedding in 1999.

sarong while on holiday – one of many 'fashion statements' that would be picked up by the Becks-hungry media.

Their wedding would take place in an 18th-century Irish castle in the summer of 1999, and only 29 guests would be invited (though another 226 would arrive to join in the later celebrations). By that time, Manchester United had achieved an historic Treble, having been crowned Premiership, FA Cup winners and European Champions. Life just couldn't get any better.

The European Cup Final had been the biggest moment of an epic season, opponents Bayern Munich having taken the lead in the sixth minute and refusing to yield an inch. So resolute was the German defence that many United fans had left the Nou Camp stadium in Barcelona as injury time approached, convinced their side would have to make do with the domestic Double. After all, it was United's third in a decade!

One minute into injury time, veteran striker Teddy Sheringham displayed all his goalpoacher's guile by deflecting a shot bound for the terraces into the net. United, tails up, pushed forward again as the Germans clung to what they had and waited for the final whistle and the seemingly inevitable extra time. But David had other ideas, and when Bayern desperately conceded a corner, swung in one of his trademark flag-kicks.

In a move perfected at the Cliff training ground, Sheringham met the ball and flicked it onto the far post. There, super substitute Ole Gunnar Solskjaer was waiting to dispatch the ball into the roof of the net. Three minutes had seen United go from a goal down to having both hands on the European Cup for the first time since 1968.

Even though England's Euro 2000 campaign failed to live up to expectation, with defeat against Romania sending them home early from the Finals, United continued to dominate the domestic scene, winning yet another Premiership title for 1999-2000 (though they lost the European Cup to Real Madrid). David's own celebrity status was confirmed when he came second to Brazilian superstar Rivaldo in the voting for World and European Player of the Year, as well as runner-up in the BBC Sports Personality of the Year.

David Beckham celebrated the new year of 2001 by splashing out on a £185,000 Lamborghini Diablo sports car to add to a fleet that already contained cars by Mercedes, Ferrari, TVR and Range Rover. "Victoria can't understand how I get so excited about things like cars," he complained good-naturedly.

There was the occasional run-in with manager Alex Ferguson, not least when he adopted a punk-style Mohican haircut. That had to go because "it wasn't fitting for a Man United player". Though popular in the United camp, these days he heads straight home after every game rather than hang around with his pals. "I like to spend as much time with my family as I can, which can be hard because Victoria and I are so busy." He also reveals Posh "gives a pretty good massage" – which would be enough to have most red-blooded males come running! **DB**

The Captain in action against Sweden in the World Cup 2002.

Captain Beckham

With a wife, son and career to die for, David Beckham had the world at his feet. But better yet was to come in 2001. Not only did United finish the 2000-2001 season on top of the pile yet again, but, after Kevin Keegan suddenly resigned as England manager, caretaker boss Peter Taylor handed David the captain's armband. The now-retired international Alan Shearer, himself a former national team captain, is just one player who believes that in David Beckham England have the very best. "He's been through a lot, and he's handled everything that's been thrown at him. Now he's captaining them well, playing well and chipping in with the odd goal."

With Becks at the helm on the field and a new manager, super Swede Sven Goran Eriksson masterminding the tactics from the sidelines, England would beat the odds, retrieve the seemingly impossible situation that had caused Keegan's resignation and book their place in the 2002 World Cup in Japan and Korea.

The matches that secured that dream ticket were a 5-1 win in Germany – an unprecedented result against the team whose slim victory at Wembley had toppled Keegan over the edge – and a last-gasp draw against Greece at Old Trafford in October that had been secured by a last-minute Beckham 'bender' of a free-kick. It seemed as if England were about to blow their chance, twice letting the Greeks take the lead and threatening to turn David's dream day – leading his country at his club's home ground – into a disaster. Fortunately, as ever, the one player with the capability to change the script did just that, and the world's headline-writers were once again putting their word processors into overdrive.

As if all that wasn't enough, he scored again against Greece – this time their top club, Olympiakos – just four days later in the Champions League. Sir Alex Ferguson had been tempted to put his star player, who had gone through an emotional rollercoaster in the past 72 hours, on the bench, but David begged to be given a place in the starting line-up. He then repaid his boss's faith by notching the opening goal in a notable win, inspiring the headline: 'Greece 0, Becks 2'. "It was a hard match on Saturday," the player admitted, "but this was a big game. I told the manager I was fine and that was all he needed to know. 'Marathon Man Becks', as the tabloids dubbed him, had done the business yet again as

United advanced to the second stage in a competition they were all desperate to win for outgoing manager Ferguson, who'd announced he was to retire at the end of the season.

By this time, Victoria had put her solo career into the fast lane, the Spice Girls having ceased trading after their notably less successful third CD release, 'Forever', in November 2000. Her first solo album 'Not Such An Innocent Girl' was released in October of the following year and immediately debuted in the Number 10 chart position. The couple made an appearance on TV's prime-time Parkinson show to promote it, causing much mirth when Victoria referred to her husband as 'Goldenballs'! That reflected back on an earlier interview where a jokey remark that David 'borrowed my underwear' led to much ribald terrace chanting. It had been a lesson that anything the 'golden couple' said would flash round the world at the speed of light. She was, she explained, proud of everything David had achieved. "It was amazing when we found out he was going to be captain of England," she said, admitting that, while she was no football expert, "I enjoy it." David, for his part, denied any wish to become a pop star. "I'll leave that to the wife. She does that well enough."

For any captain, a looming World Cup campaign is a stressful time. But when it's questionable if you'll play at all, the pressure and impending disappointment is immense. After the seriousness of David's injury (sustained while playing against Deportivo La Curuna late in the 2001-2002 European Champions League season,) was revealed doubts began to rise as to whether David would be fit to play against Sweden in England's opening match. The last few weeks leading up to the World Cup were spent in treatment, taking light exercise.

Facing the press at England's training ground he told reporters that he was fit to play – and he was definitely ready to lead England. Beckham's attitude since that fateful night in 1998 against Argentina had changed, and he was ready to face Diego Simeone once more. Turn to page 48 to read about the highlights of that incredible match. **DB**

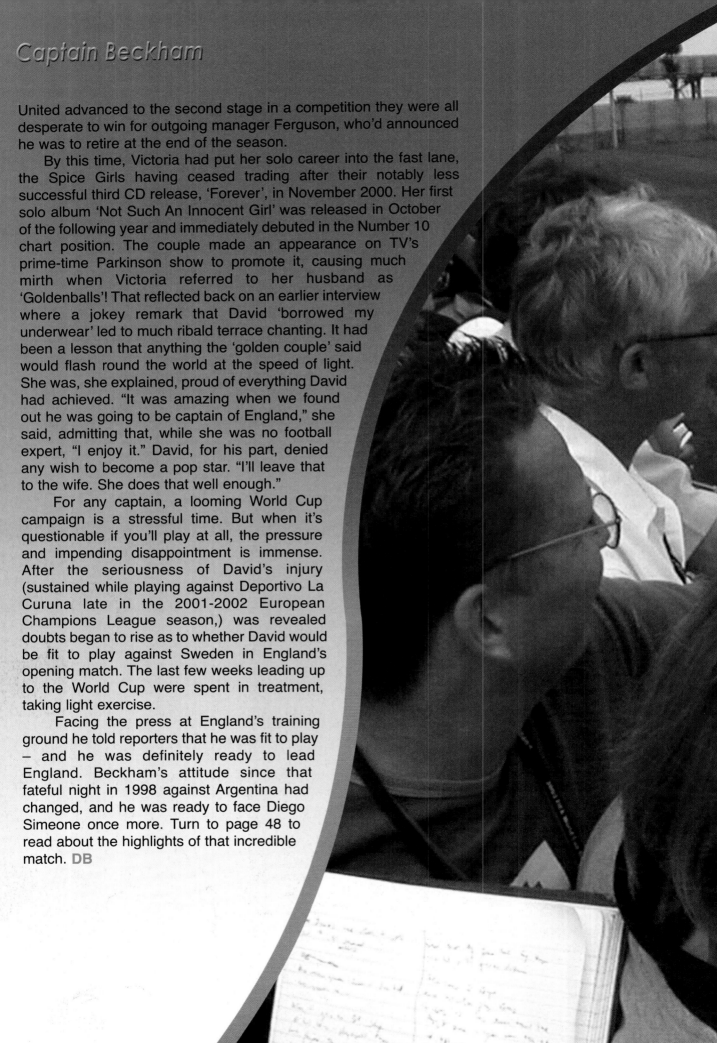

Captain Beckham

David faces the press as England prepare for their vital World Cup matches in 2002.

Beckham QUIZ

So you think you're a Beckham expert? Find out how much you really know about the England captain with a quick quiz. Check your answers on page 34.

1. What is Beckham's full name?

2. Where was David born?

3. Who did David score against from the penalty spot in the World Cup 2002?

4. What name does David have tattooed on his back?

5. Who was in charge of England when David was announced as England captain?

6. What is the name of David Beckham's manager at Manchester United?

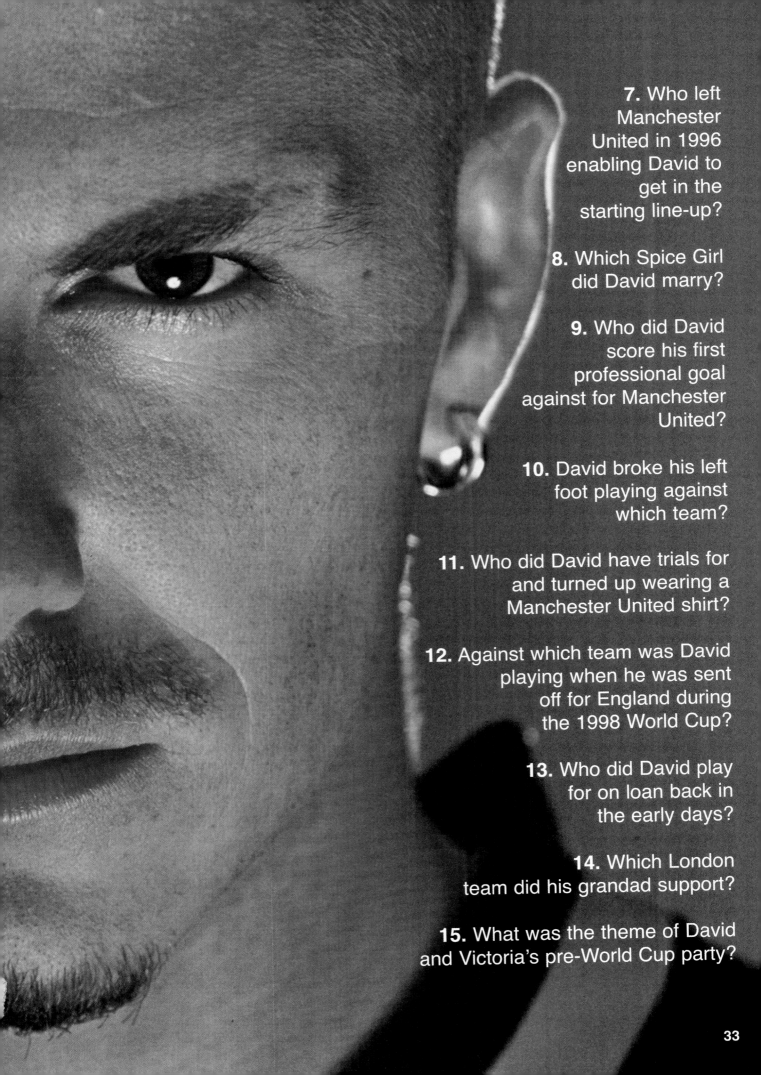

7. Who left Manchester United in 1996 enabling David to get in the starting line-up?

8. Which Spice Girl did David marry?

9. Who did David score his first professional goal against for Manchester United?

10. David broke his left foot playing against which team?

11. Who did David have trials for and turned up wearing a Manchester United shirt?

12. Against which team was David playing when he was sent off for England during the 1998 World Cup?

13. Who did David play for on loan back in the early days?

14. Which London team did his grandad support?

15. What was the theme of David and Victoria's pre-World Cup party?

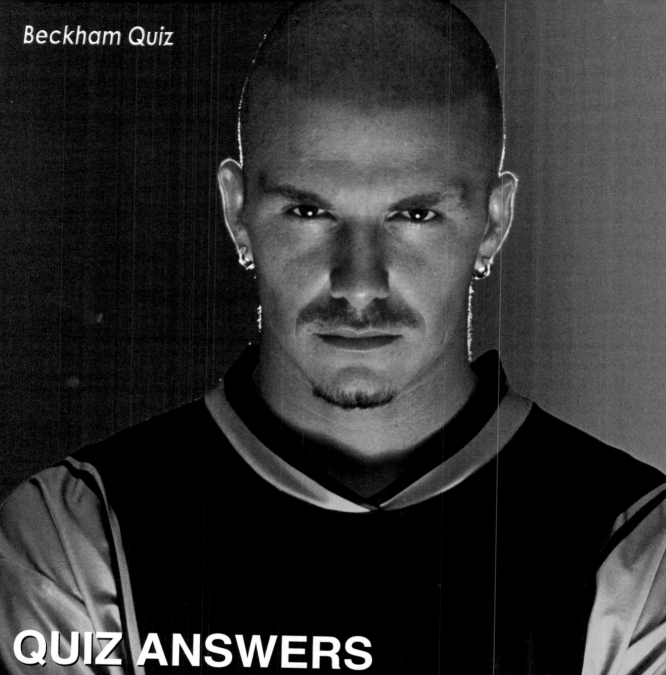

QUIZ ANSWERS

Check your answers below and see how much of a Beckham fanatic you are.

1. David Robert Joseph Beckham   2. Leytonstone, East London
3. Argentina   4. Brooklyn   5. Peter Taylor   6. Alex Ferguson
7. Andrei Kanchelskis   8. Posh Spice - Victoria Adams   9. Galatasary
10. Deportivo La Coruna   11. Tottenham Hotspurs   12. Argentina
13. Preston North End   14. Tottenham Hotspurs   15. Japanese

Beckham in action against Denmark.

Action Gallery

Beckham in action against Sweden in the opening match of England's World Cup 2002 campaign.

England beat
the Argentines
with this spot-kick
from Beckham,
World Cup
2002 campaign.

Action Gallery

37

Being Beckham

So you want to be David Beckham? Well, hard luck – as the song goes, there's only one! What you can do, though, is take a few tips from the master and make the best of the skills you've been given. It takes a lot of blood, sweat and tears to be a superstar… but if David can do it, why can't you?

One special piece of assistance that wasn't around when Becks was young is a computer game, David Beckham Soccer, which lets you access many of his training tips via the screen of Xbox, Playstation 2 or Game Boy. But even that's no substitute for getting out there with a ball and doing it yourself.

When interviewed by the Dreem Teem on BBC Radio One in May 2002, Becks revealed that when they picked teams at school he was always the last to be selected. "I used to get booted everywhere because I was really little," he said. The kids only changed their minds after David went to the Bobby Charlton Soccer School and got himself in the papers. So if that's not the incentive you need to persevere, don't bother reading any further!

When discussing his future plans earlier in 2002, David revealed he might even start his own soccer school. "I have always enjoyed working with kids. I don 't see myself becoming a television pundit or a manager, but the idea of working with youngsters appeals to me." Until that moment arrives – and you can form a queue over there! – we offer these tips to better football. The story of the next David Beckham could start here…

Perseverance

David himself puts his footballing skills down to hours of continuous practice and training. When he was young, he would work with his Dad and on his own in the local park until late in the evening. Even now, Beckham relentlessly practises his art. His skills are the result of long hours spent honing those trademark free-kicks and shooting on the training pitch.

Equipment

Your boots should be light, well fitting and in good condition (oh, and don't forget shin pads!). David promotes and wears Adidas Predator Precision boots, which are claimed to increase accuracy and precision, providing players with even greater power and control than normal boots. Even Brooklyn has a miniature pair – but be warned, full-size ones cost £300!

Being Beckham

Get Proper Training

Beckham was a star pupil at the Bobby Charlton Soccer School, where he learned many vital skills between the ages of 11 and 13. If a local league club has a football in the community scheme, sign up and be prepared to learn. It beats kicking a ball against a wall, encourages teamwork – and, if you've got what it takes, you might just get noticed by a scout.

Open Your Eyes

The fact David once scored from the half-way line (in the first game of the 1996/97 season at Wimbledon) shows not only his shooting accuracy but his eye for a half-chance. Your awareness of the possibilities open to you can be enhanced by watching as much football as possible when not playing yourself.

Stamina Shows

Few players today can equal Beckham's exceptional reserves of stamina and physical fitness. He is full of energy right to the final whistle. This is a result of regular training and a suitable diet. A good diet is important – eat regular meals, with plenty of carbohydrates (pasta, etc) before games, stay away from chocolate and crisps. But don't worry about high-priced energy drinks; a good supply of water is perfectly adequate.

Banana Tricks

Bending or swerving the ball is a Beckham trademark. This skill can be used in many areas, such as scoring shots around a defensive wall, corner kicks, crosses into the box and passing the ball around opponents. You use the outside of the foot to swerve the ball away from you, or the inside of the foot to bend the ball inwards. Practise this with friends making up a defensive wall – or if your friends have given up and gone home, try wheeliebins!

Have Heroes

David idolised old players like Glenn Hoddle, Bryan Robson and Bobby Charlton, and even now believes that "if I can reach their level I will be happy." So even if you're too old to have posters on the bedroom wall, choose a role model and use them to motivate you when the whole world seems against you. We know one with the initials DB, in case you need a suggestion…

Don't Give Up

It may be hard to believe now, but David was once a skinny kid, rejected by the England Schoolboys for his lack of height. But in time he found he had the physique to match his silky skills. Everyone develops physically at their own rate – so don't despair if the opposition is bigger than you, you may yet catch up with them.

Don't Be a Big Head

Despite his great gifts, David's always kept both feet firmly on the ground. "I never used to think I was the best – I just used to concentrate on my game." So don't let success spoil you; remember that even superstars like Becks are still training, still learning and will be until they hang up their Predator boots!

Take Advice

Bobby Charlton told the 12-year-old Becks to "shoot at all times if you've got a chance" – and that's just one piece of good advice he's used to his advantage over the years. You can play football with your eyes, feet and ears too – so keep listening for some handy hints and tips from those in the know.

Play With the Big Boys

Becks was put up an age group when he was younger, and proved he could cut it with older kids by rising to the top in his new environment. If you need a challenge, then play with people older than yourself – you'll toughen up quickly and could just learn a few new tricks!

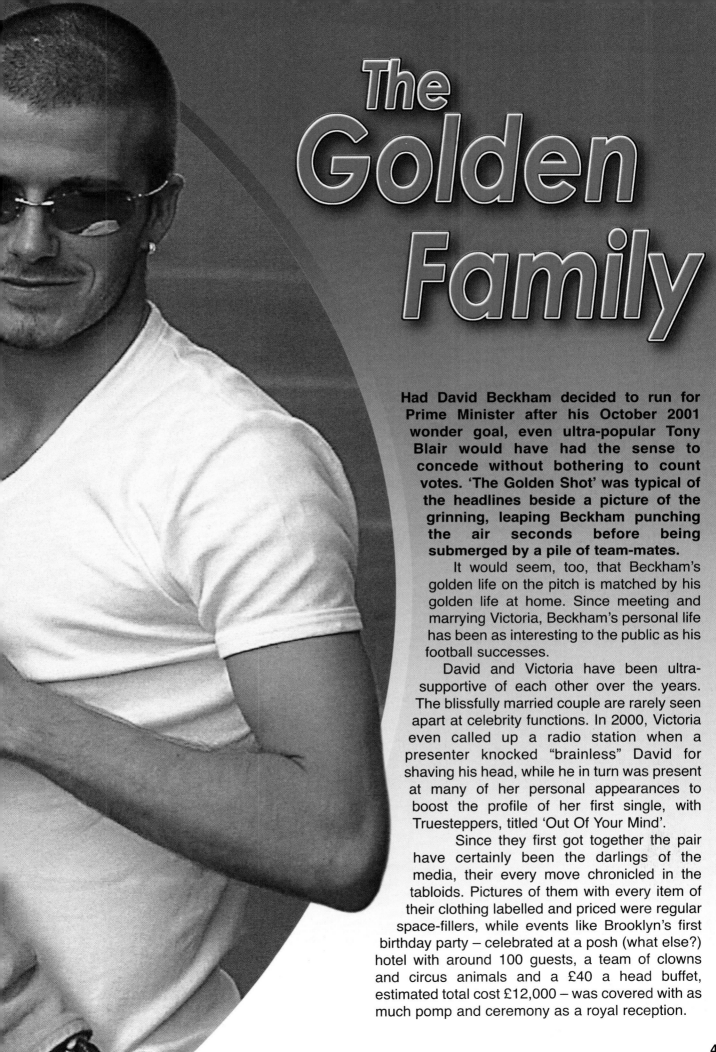

The Golden Family

Had David Beckham decided to run for Prime Minister after his October 2001 wonder goal, even ultra-popular Tony Blair would have had the sense to concede without bothering to count votes. 'The Golden Shot' was typical of the headlines beside a picture of the grinning, leaping Beckham punching the air seconds before being submerged by a pile of team-mates.

It would seem, too, that Beckham's golden life on the pitch is matched by his golden life at home. Since meeting and marrying Victoria, Beckham's personal life has been as interesting to the public as his football successes.

David and Victoria have been ultra-supportive of each other over the years. The blissfully married couple are rarely seen apart at celebrity functions. In 2000, Victoria even called up a radio station when a presenter knocked "brainless" David for shaving his head, while he in turn was present at many of her personal appearances to boost the profile of her first single, with Truesteppers, titled 'Out Of Your Mind'.

Since they first got together the pair have certainly been the darlings of the media, their every move chronicled in the tabloids. Pictures of them with every item of their clothing labelled and priced were regular space-fillers, while events like Brooklyn's first birthday party – celebrated at a posh (what else?) hotel with around 100 guests, a team of clowns and circus animals and a £40 a head buffet, estimated total cost £12,000 – was covered with as much pomp and ceremony as a royal reception.

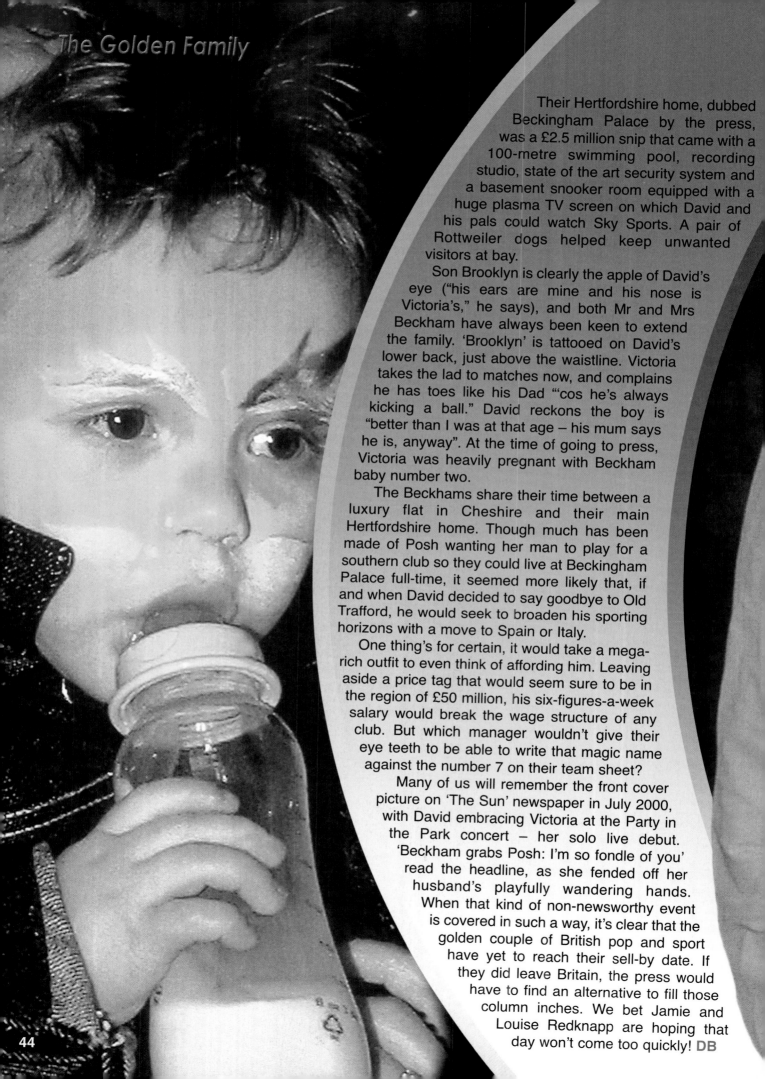

Their Hertfordshire home, dubbed Beckingham Palace by the press, was a £2.5 million snip that came with a 100-metre swimming pool, recording studio, state of the art security system and a basement snooker room equipped with a huge plasma TV screen on which David and his pals could watch Sky Sports. A pair of Rottweiler dogs helped keep unwanted visitors at bay.

Son Brooklyn is clearly the apple of David's eye ("his ears are mine and his nose is Victoria's," he says), and both Mr and Mrs Beckham have always been keen to extend the family. 'Brooklyn' is tattooed on David's lower back, just above the waistline. Victoria takes the lad to matches now, and complains he has toes like his Dad "'cos he's always kicking a ball." David reckons the boy is "better than I was at that age – his mum says he is, anyway". At the time of going to press, Victoria was heavily pregnant with Beckham baby number two.

The Beckhams share their time between a luxury flat in Cheshire and their main Hertfordshire home. Though much has been made of Posh wanting her man to play for a southern club so they could live at Beckingham Palace full-time, it seemed more likely that, if and when David decided to say goodbye to Old Trafford, he would seek to broaden his sporting horizons with a move to Spain or Italy.

One thing's for certain, it would take a mega-rich outfit to even think of affording him. Leaving aside a price tag that would seem sure to be in the region of £50 million, his six-figures-a-week salary would break the wage structure of any club. But which manager wouldn't give their eye teeth to be able to write that magic name against the number 7 on their team sheet?

Many of us will remember the front cover picture on 'The Sun' newspaper in July 2000, with David embracing Victoria at the Party in the Park concert – her solo live debut. 'Beckham grabs Posh: I'm so fondle of you' read the headline, as she fended off her husband's playfully wandering hands. When that kind of non-newsworthy event is covered in such a way, it's clear that the golden couple of British pop and sport have yet to reach their sell-by date. If they did leave Britain, the press would have to find an alternative to fill those column inches. We bet Jamie and Louise Redknapp are hoping that day won't come too quickly! **DB**

World Cup 2002 review

Captaining his country had certainly had an effect on David Beckham, but even for someone as level-headed as he is, the weight of expectation as England approached the World Cup 2002 was immense. 'We've got a very hard group," he insisted. "You need a certain amount of luck especially in a big competition like the World Cup. If you get through the first few stages you've a good chance."

People had suggested an England team with untried youngsters like the Coles, Joe and Ashley, might be a better bet for the World Cup in Germany in four years time, but David disagreed. "Some have said it's too early for us to do well in a big competition, but I don't think it is. People had a go at the Man United manager when he bunged us youngsters in..." Enough said!

Sunday June 2

ENGLAND 1 - 1 SWEDEN

Fortunately, Becks was pronounced fit after his seven and a half weeks lay-off to win his 50th cap in the showdown against Sweden in Saitama. But coach Sven Goran Eriksson elected not to risk his other 'crocked' midfielders, Nicky Butt and Keiron Dyer. Kick-off at home was 12.30pm, late at night in the Far East which gave the England players some respite from the heat.

And they pleased the watching millions by turning on a different kind of heat against the Swedes, eight of whom played their club football in the English Premiership. It was no suprise when central defender Sol Campbell put the stresses and strains of a Double-winning season behind him, powering upfield to head home a corner by...who else? David did his own corner-flag celebration as the others rushed to hug the scorer.

But it was no coincidence that, as the captain tired in the second half, the initiative was lost. Everton's Alexandersson equalised, the Swedes finished stronger and David was withdrawn not long after the hour mark to give him a rest and keep him fresh for the upcoming battle with Argentina, six days away. His foot had come through its first test, all was well – and, as he remarked, at least England hadn't lost their first game, a situation that would have made the Argentina game even more of a pressure match.

Up against Super Swede
Fredrick Ljunberg in
England's opening match.

1st ROUND
- match 2

ARGENTINA 0 - 1 ENGLAND

One summer Friday afternoon in Sapporo, a single kick of the ball from David Beckham undid all the damage of his infamous kick on an opponent four years earlier and gave England every chance of proceeding to the second phase of the World Cup 2002. His penalty gave England the narrowest of wins against old enemies Argentina, revenging defeats in 1998 (David's dismissal) and 1986, the latter the famous Maradona match where an illegal 'hand of God' goal sent England home from Mexico empty-handed. And just as importantly for the immediate future, he'd played the full 90 minutes.

The whole country had come to a standstill at 12.30pm local time on 7th June, hoping against hope that Sven's men could start better than they had finished against his native Swedes a few short days earlier. And they were rewarded; the team kept their heads as fair and foul tackles thundered in, England defending so resolutely that star men Veron, Bastituta and Gonzales proved ineffective and were substituted. Michael Owen, who won the penalty just before half-time, had come close to notching another England goal, but the South Americans' heads went down and, though there were nailbiting moments, it always seemed that one might be enough to secure at least a share of the points.

Afterwards, the captain and goalscorer was understandably the centre of attention. Knowing he would be on front as well as the back pages, David remained commendably dignified in victory. And even though the Argentines had done their best to put him off converting the penalty, he made a point of shaking old enemy Simeone's hand after the game. It was left to others back home to lavish praise. "David was different class," said his predecessor as England captain, Alan Shearer. "What a leader, what a man he is. He struck the penalty as if he was playing in the park."

What David's coolness had ensured was that England need only a draw with Nigeria to progress.

Beckham sprints away in delight after scoring England's only goal, from the penalty spot, against Argentina.

1st ROUND
- match 3

Wednesday June 12

NIGERIA 0 - 0 ENGLAND

If ever a match could be called a banana skin, this was it. Lose to Nigeria, already out but with pride to play for, and the heroics against Argentina might all be in vain. Happily, it didn't happen as things turned out, a 1-0 defeat would still have let England through - so a relatively subdued David led the team through 90 goalless minutes that let Nigeria break their duck and gave England the point they needed to be safe.

Schools and offices had opened early to let pupils and workers watch the match round communal TVs - and, though the game hadn't been much to get out of bed for, no-one was complaining. Even better, Sweden's draw with Argentina sent Veron, Bastituta and company scuttling miserably back to South America. - "It's been such an unpredictable World Cup so far, you can't pick a winner," said England coach Sven Goran Eriksson, reflecting that holders France had also been dispatched empty-handed. Too late - thousands of people home on the other side of the world already had picked a winner in their minds. And they wore the Three Lions on their shirt! Yet the anti-climax of the Nigeria game was enough to bring a much-needed sense of reality to proceedings, balancing fans' expectations.

Second in their group behind the Swedes, England had avoided the dangerous Senegal in the first knock-out phase, instead drawing more familiar faces of Denmark. Only problem was... should they beat the Danes, mighty Brazil would be next to bar their path to glory. Still, for England and David Beckham, surely nothing was impossible!

Beckham does some fancy footwork against Nigeria.

✚ DENMARK — 0 - 3 — ENGLAND ✚✚

Back in traditional white, Sven's men had a dream start to the knockout phase. Since England's two goals in the tournament so far had stemmed from set plays, it wasn't surprising they opened their account against Denmark from another Beckham corner. This time it was Rio Ferdinand who rose to head home, aided by an uncharacteristic fumble from Sunderland keeper Thomas Sorensen. And this in the first five minutes!

But even better was to come a quarter of an hour later when England's other Golden Boy Michael Owen finally came good - much to the obvious delight of his team-mates. A left-wing cross from Trevor Sinclair, a great success in the problem midfield position, was flicked on by Butt and that was enough for Owen to pounce. "The door to the quarter finals is definitely ajar!" jubilant John Motson informed the watching millions as the players hugged - and the 10,000 England fans in the stadium at Niigata clearly felt the same. As half-time approached. and box-watchers at home prepared to put on the kettle, David played a part in putting the game beyond the Danes. Picking up a quick Danny Mills throw, he slid the ball square for Emile Hesky to slip his shot off the rain-soaked pitch and under Sorensen.

With the game all but won, Sven shuffled the pack and brought on Fowler, Dyer and Sheringham. But though there was little to get him off his pitchside seat, David managed to bother Sorenson with a couple of testing shots.

Denmark's Jensen came closest to another goal. The hugs at the end were genuine enough, many of the red-shirted Danes being familiar Premiership faces, but more exotic opposition awaited... From 14-1 outsiders when the World Cup kicked off, England were now 7-2 second favourites behind - Brazil!

Michael Owen celebrates the goal by Rio Ferdinand and England are on their way. Next stop Brazil!

QUARTER FINAL

⊞⊞ ENGLAND 1 - 2 BRAZIL ◉

The whole country stopped in its tracks on Friday morning 21st June to witness a match all agreed would have been the perfect World Cup Final. The Samba Boys from Rio were to meet Beckham's boys from England - not forgetting our own Rio! - and something would have give. Naturally, everyone hoped the game would be a footballing spectacle... but with the right result.

And that possibility looked very much on when Michael Owen pounced on a Brazilian defensive mistake by unlucky Lucio to slot the ball home after 20 minutes. This was the dream start England had hoped for, and the tails visibly went up in the stifling heat of Shizuoka. The Beckham-esque cross-field ball that set it up had been supplied by Emile Heskey, of all people, and he like his team-mates was playing out of his skin.

To have come in a goal up would have set England for a great second half. But it was not to be. Keeper David Seaman had injured his back reaching for a cross and, in the time added on, Rivaldo added to his record of scoring in every game by slotting home a Ronaldino through ball with his magical left foot.

And it was Ronaldino who undid England just a few minutes into the second half. His floated set-piece fooled Seaman and cannoned in off the underside of the bar at the far post. To lose to Brazilian skill was one thing - a probable fluke goal was another matter!

Even a sending-off that gave England a man advantage proved insufficient and, despite David's on-field leadership and the introduction of three substitutes to replace tired legs, the task proved too great. David had required touchline treatment for a foot injury but had played on regardless, determined to earn his place in the roll call of English heroes. Sadly, the men in white shirts were to return home without the trophy, but their teamwork and spirit promised much for the years to come.

Below, Michael Owen scores England's goal and then celebrates with David Beckham and Danny Mills (right).

The moment which put England out! The ball looped over David Seaman and into the back of the net.

Considering Beckham's appearance in the tournament at all was touch and go for awhile, he could look back on World Cup 2002 as a personal triumph. Apart from one game, he'd played each and every minute of England's campaign, and rarely seemed troubled by either the heat or his previously broken foot.

Though Victoria had been unable to fly out with the rest of the wives and girlfriends, being too heavily pregnant with the second Baby Beckham, there would be a few short weeks to enjoy each other's company before the start of the new Premiership season. With Roy Keane's footballing future up in the air after his depature from the Eire squad on the eve of the World Cup, there was even the possibility that David could eventually captain his club as well as his country. And that, along with the safe delivery of his offspring-to-be, would surely be the final piece of his dream.

Celebrations after the defeat of Argentina

Campbell scores England's first World Cup goal against Sweden.

The midfield maestro in action against Denmark in the 2nd Round game.

YES! 3-0 and onto the next round. Beckham and Heskey celebrate the 3rd goal against Denmark.

Beckham Phenomenon

Well Beckham fans, we hope you've enjoyed the David Beckham Annual and learned a lot about the great man himself. You can be sure there is more to come in the following years. But before you go, have a look at these fascinating facts.

The Game Boy Advance computer system has signed David to star as a cartoon character in the game Go Go Beckham. 'I always dreamed of being a superhero when I was younger' admitted Becks.

Beckham originally wore the Number 10 shirt at United, inheriting the Number 7 shirt vacated by Eric Cantona when Teddy Sheringham joined the club.

David scored his first goal in the Champions League against Galatasaray in 1994, in the Premiership against Aston Villa in 1995 and in the FA Cup against Chelsea in 1996. His first international goal was scored against Colombia in World Cup '98.

David has son Brooklyn's name tattooed on his lower back, a large angel on his upper back and his wife's name Victoria (spelled incorrectly) in Hindi tattooed on his arm.

When David scored the equaliser against Chelsea on 22 February 1997, the speed of his shot was measured at 97.9 mph.

David first captained the England team on 15 November 2000 in a friendly against Italy, having served as vice captain for the previous two internationals. It was manager Peter Taylor's only game in charge.

David scored two goals, against Doncaster and Fulham, in the five games he played on loan with Third Division Preston North End in 1994-95. That season he also scored for United in the Champions League.

The study of David Beckham is part of a 12-week 'football culture' module for a Degree course at Staffordshire University.

Beckham Phenomenon

David wears a new pair of Predator boots every game he plays in at an estimated cost of £300 a pair!

A recent experiment showed that Beckham runs an average of 8.8 miles per game - more than any other player in the United team.

David supported the Red Devils as a boy, following his father Ted's example, and once turned up for a trial at Tottenham wearing a United kit.

David Beckham is currently reckoned to be worth a cool £20 million. He lives in a £2.5 million house in Hertfordshire and has sponsorship deals with Adidas, Pepsi and Brylcreem. His new deal with United is rumoured to be costing the club £90,000 a week.

A foot-high gold statue of David has been placed in Bangkok's Pariwas Buddhist Temple alongside 100 effigies of minor gods. A sculptor named Thongruang Haemhod supposedly made the idol to keep Beckham's memory alive for the next thousand years.

Until next year...

With his second child due in September 2002, David Beckham is in a win/win situation: a sporting superstar whose life off the field is as successful as his on-pitch activities. Despite tempting offers at home and abroad, he seems destined to spend the rest of his career playing for Manchester United, the club he followed as a boy.

As captain of England, he's turned the hate and disapproval of jealous fans of rival clubs into love and respect, showing a remarkable humility despite his amazing gifts. He's the boy next door done good, and there are plenty of chapters to his success story yet to be written. Watch this space!